Muhammad's Beard

Muhammad's Beard

ISBN: 978-1-105-24288-5

Dedication

To your third cousin's
twice removed step daughter's
uncle's brother in law.

Contents

Foreword

I have known the author for at least one week and would like to take this opportunity to controvert the despicable lies that have recently surfaced.

He is not, nor has he ever had any affiliation with, or inclination to be a nazi, neo-nazi, nationalist or member of the Conservative Party. Nor is he a jew, muslim, hinduist, fundamental christian, atheist or fishmonger.

He does, however, owe me £60 and if he refuses to return this generous loan I shall be forced to break his ankles.

Professor Cedric Elizabeth Smith

B.A., M.A., Ph.D., Skateboarder

VALENTINE'S DAY

The statistics were self-evident, the conclusion beyond doubt. Semus O'Flagerty ofThe Counterpart Research Company, Bangor, Gwynedd, Wales, had, to his co-workers jubilation, uncovered the single most elusive factor previously unknown to mankind.

He, together with the support of several hundred medical researchers, bio chemists, statisticians, anthropologists and geneticists had found something that would change the world forever.

Hidden within the DNA of every living human being, Semus had discovered and decoded the irrefutable signature of marital compatibility.

The process of 'matching' was laughably simple. The smallest particle of organic material was all that was required. Once analysed the prospective client was given an eleven figure number. All that remained was to find another with a corresponding number within a range of 5000 and the perfect match of mental, emotional and physical harmony was guaranteed.

The time consuming part had been the collection and collation of all the individual genetic codes into a newly created Database of Worldwide Compatibility, which by decree was made freely accessible.

In less than 5 years and with the eager cooperation of governments worldwide, pressured by the enthusiastic support and electoral demands thrust upon them, over 90% of the worlds population had been decoded, collated and matched.

Furthermore it was soon discovered that among the billions of people that inhabit the earth there was only one perfect match for every individual, thus preventing the issue of choice from complicating the worldwide pairing process.

In countries where oppression and religious mores prevented the open practice of matching, an active underground network was quickly established, samples taken, secretly analysed and the appropriate partner revealed.

Some countries, in an effort to promote domestic harmony, forcibly imposed matching upon its population and while initially there had been fierce resistance, in the majority of cases it quickly subsided.

The earliest impact of the discovery had been the inevitable slew of divorces while millions of existing couples broke up to be united with their perfect love match.

Mass migration soon followed, since many of the matches spanned the diverse regions of the globe. Thankfully the majority of governments agreed to open their borders to anyone seeking a match who was indigenous.

Controversially matching did not work between members of the same sex, however the gay community was soon placated with the discovery that, when paired with an ideal match of the opposite sex, their previous romantic inclinations altogether disappeared, sated as they now were with hitherto unimagined harmony.

Inevitably matching still had its detractors. Among them were those who objected to the infamous pairing of 87 year old Beatrice Clavicol from Tavistock, England, with the diminutive 11 year old Aldolfo Pizzaro of Santa Clara de Nanay, Peru. This was later revealed to be a programming error and in due course the invention of home matching kits, combined with the discovery that the matching process only worked on those of a post-pubescent age, ensured the occurrence of such mishaps was reduced to a minimum.

Quite soon it was discovered that the children of matched couples were genetically and mentally far superior than the offspring of their unmatched counterparts, a large number of which remained in defiance and formed secret, violent, resistance groups.

To protect themselves, the governments of the matched masses formed themselves into a worldwide coalition, which later evolved into what was latterly named The Fourth Reich. As time past the ensuing conflicts escalated among the outer fringes of society, ultimately culminating in World Wars 3, 4, 5 and 6 and the almost total annihilation of mankind.

Semus O'Flagerty, due to an extremely rare genetic disorder, never found his perfect match and died alone aged 83. His last words were reported to have been "I only wanted to be loved."

New Years Day

Mr Pinkerton took a swig, it was to be the last swig of the year, his last swig of any year.

As soon as the bells rang and the new year announced, as soon as the bellowing crowds toasted and jeered, the fireworks blasted and cheap chinese paper lanterns released, Mr E. Pinkerton of Lower Morton was resolved (resolve being a trait Mr Pinkerton possessed in abundance, together with a fanatical aversion to chaffing, squatting and peas) to never again let another alcoholic drink pass his lips. From this day forward he would only imbibe class A drugs.

Within the top breast pocket of Mr Ernest Pinkerton's green cotton, elbow-less jacket (the cut of which had been fixed by a resolution of several years previous) poked the crisp, lined notepaper upon which the remainder of his yearly intentions had been carefully inscribed.

Among that extensive list, some bear closer inspection:

Humming - There is a time and place for humming and due to repeated beatings Ernest had, with some considerable reluctance, finally acknowledged that to do so incessantly, whilst being spoken to, was neither the time, nor the place. From this day hence he would instead look wistfully skywards whilst in conversation.

Gurning - Ernest Pinkerton's habit of gurning during sexual intimacies had, much to his own distress, resulted in the dissolution of his marriage to his long suffering and somewhat naive wife, Harriet. Indeed the former Mrs H. Pinkerton had for some years maintained the mistaken belief that gurning was a necessary prerequisite for conception and had therefore awkwardly practised the same disturbing habit in return. Only after confiding with several of her closest friends did she discover that to gurn was not in fact the secret of a happy and fruitful union.

What Hut Monthly - Ernest had decided that the subscription to this particular periodical was an extravagant and unnecessary expense. Furthermore, due to illness, he had failed to secure issue 16 which sported the second door hinge of the magazine's main attraction - on the front of each issue was packed one part of a full sized replica of a Turkish Yurt. To the exacting Mr Pinkerton this omission could not be ignored and rendered the whole project completely pointless.

With regard to the aforementioned non consumption of alcohol, that particular commitment was not entirely of his own violation, or rather it was a consequence of one other resolution written precisely 335 days earlier, upon the very same notepaper within his top pocket.

It read thus: "I shall from this day forth, on the purchase of an alcoholic drink, preform a nazi salute.

And I shall accompany said salute with the loud cry of 'Your mother is a donkey bollock'."

Naturally this did not sit well in the liberal district of Lower Morton, Wessex, England, nor for that matter in any of the public houses he had frequented during the course of the past year. And so it was, that at the stroke of 12, Mr Ernest Pinkerton once again found himself sprawled unconscious before yet another bar.

Muhammad's Beard

"Oooo, ohhh, ugh, arrgh, oooo, eeeyerr, hmmmm, eeoooyoor..." A hand slipped gently under the hoodless karakul burka. Pinching hard she grasped buttock and thigh. Squealing with delight she was answered by the light nip of earlobe between heavy, moist lips. It had been a good day. A monumental day.

Three floors below, the conference hummed with the birth of a new dawn. A dawn of peace, unthinkable, yet present.

Forty point two years earlier, an entirely different monumental event was gestating within the dried up womb of the Middle East. It started with a beating.

A certain Mr Wasim Jabbar of Emamverdi Street, Tehran, was somewhat miffled about his betrothed's less than enthusiastic approach to his so called conjugal rights. He was beginning to suspect that the endless migraines were a ruse. Furthermore there was something very inconvenient about the timing of her menstrual cycle. Suffice to say, Wasim was a very frustrated Muslim, hence the beating.

On that particular night Wasim went too far and Mrs Sabah Jabbar kicked the shit out of his inconsiderate Islamically indoctrinated body. Excrement flew skywards, together with an unhealthy dose of blood. An iron fire-poker helped. Still, for a young lady, she packed a mighty whack.

A new name, a new country and a new burka, Sabah unearthed an inner strength the equivalent of her bicepital prowess. The Iranian authorities believed she had been kidnapped by violent criminals and it was beyond the imagination of the few ageing family members to suspect otherwise. She was free.

In the chaos that was Baghdad, she found a hostel and a menial job within the Ministry of State for Women's Affairs, cleaning toilets. Within three years she was aide to the chief minister. After a further four she was the leader of Muslim Action for Women's Liberation, a group of radical females devoted to the destruction of religious prejudice and male oppression.

It was Sabah's idea to use sex as their main tool of attrition. If men wouldn't lay off, they wouldn't lay down, lie back, shut up or submit. National No Burka Day and Kebabless Sunday were other methods used in their struggle.

During the following years of beatings, riots, prison and martyrdom, MAWL had attained several positions within the government, securing many of the rights which western women took for granted.

Was it Sabah who was responsible for these stupendous changes? In part yes. Sabah represented the spearhead. A new generation was taking control, a generation tired of outdated bigotry and fearful doctrines. Thirty years after beating her husband to death, she was elected to be the first female president ever to grace any Islamic country.

Sabah's first Arab-Israeli initiative was an abject failure. Few members of the Arab League were prepared to accept any compromise, especially since its author was a woman. The Syrians were particularly incalcitrant, officially stating "We don't want no god damned woman poking her fat nose in man's business, gerrouta here!"

Moustapha Ali Khan's archeological discovery of the century would alter history forever. During excavations in the outskirts of Mecca, he uncovered a collection of over 900 parchment scrolls. Carbon dated to the 7th century AD they comprised of letters and discourses between the Prophet Muhammad's Shabbah*, together with the first drafts of several of the Quran's surah**.

Among the startling revelations were strange references to the renaming of a woman named Muhibbah. Any depiction of the Prophet's face was to be explicity forbidden. Other letters mentioned false beards and jockstraps. The conclusion left Moustapha Ali Khan fearful for his life. Muhammad was a woman.

It was several years before the Islamic world finally accepted the incontrovertible proof that the Prophet was a male impersonator.

It was another several years later that Sabah was ordained the first Caliph† since the abolition of the Ottoman Sultanate in 1924.

With the now obligatory backing of every member of the Arab League, negotiations between Jew and Arab proceeded tentatively. Israeli-Palestinian territorial claims and counter claims were the inevitable stumbling block and neither the ageing Sabah, nor the newly elected Israeli President Shona Meir were prepared to compromise.

An inaugural summit for the conclusion of Israeli-Palestinian affairs was scheduled. After much wrangling it was agreed that the Bahamas would provide an ideal location. In an effort to speed up the dialogue, Caliph Sabah and President Shona were to meet informally at the luxurious Dendabourne Conference Centre, Three Mile Hill, St. Michael.

Was it the dazzling aquamarine sea? Perhaps it was the gentle surf, lapping the soft, white sand? Or maybe it was the faint, primitive beat of reggae music, wafting over the cool trade winds. Whatever it was, Sabah and Shona fell instantly in love.

The Delegates from both sides were naturally stupefied by the sudden amicability shown between the two previously fractious leaders. As the summit progressed the coy smiles, lingering gazes and lengthy handshakes did nothing to ease their confusion.

What they were sure of was the new force with which both Sabah and Shona were advocating compromise and reconciliation.

A rigorous programme of appeasement was implemented by which interfaith marriage was rewarded with huge financial incentives. Disputed lands were occupied by non-partisan families of both

Jewish and Muslim faiths. September the 18th was designated RamKipur, a rough midpoint of Ramadan and the Jewish day of atonement, Yom Kippur. Violence was punishable by tickling.

It is a testament to the success of their initiative that within four years of interbreeding, peace was finally restored in the Middle East.

All this was forgotten three floors above the celebratory conference. In secret they kissed, they swooned, they scissored. Reaching for Sabah's sagging, wrinkled bosom, Shona bent forward and broke wind.

"Eee, you're right cheeky you are," whispered the Caliph in reply.

*Shabbah - Muhammad's companions.
**Surah - Chapters of the Quran.
†Caliph - Leader of the community of Islam.

Christmas Day

"Who by worrying can add an inch to his height."
Matthew 6:27-29

Christmas Day 0 AD was a sombre affair. Nobody turned up. Not even Jesus. This was because he wasn't born on Christmas Day.

For a dwarf, Jesus was an exceptional fellow. At the age of 2, his ability to lift enormously heavy pieces of timber was the first sign of a remarkable future. His wispy black beard was another.

He did have faults. On being instructed by his father to construct a 5 x 10 oak lowboy, he instead proceeded to lathe 300 cedar egg cups. On questioning his disobedience, Jesus replied "Let him who is without egg cups cast the first stone." Clearly his knack for the parable needed development and Mr Joseph Ben Heli duly sent him off to the Essenic School of Allegory, Qumran.

It was the Essene's practice to allegorise everything. For example, at the dinner table, the act of passing condiments may be initiated with the phrase, "If my lentils have lost their saltiness, how can they be made salty again?" Or when in need of the toilet, "It is not that which comes out of the bottom; but that which comes out of the mouth, that defiles a man."

Many Essene rituals have been lost in time. A particular favourite of Jesus was the juggling of fish and buns (this talent was to be much misrepresented by future chroniclers). They were also accomplished songsmiths, the earliest known version of 'Kumbaya' being sung among the local caves, which afforded superb acoustics.

Architecturally the Essene's were less proficient. Modern archeologists mistake the low, broken walls and roofless enclosures as the eroded shadows of once complete buildings. In reality they have been perfectly preserved under layers of wind swept sand and represent the communities exact living conditions. It was for this reason that Jesus ended his training, complaining bitterly, "My feet are as the frozen bollocks of a monkey."

The raising of Lazarus is a testament to his superb medical training. There has been much confusion over this story, the majority of reports stating the poor chap was dead. Dead drunk would be more accurate. It was Jesus's incisive diagnosis and application of herbal remedies (a precursor to Resolve™) that led to his rapid recovery.

It is a fact that Jesus never walked on water, though he was an expert swimmer and five times winner of the Gallilean 200m toe-stroke, the highest splash for a bomb and the 20 metre belly-flop. These aquatic achievements were rewarded with a small bronze trophy, latterly mistaken for the holy grail.

In future years many so called Christians would be persecuted and thrown to the lions, when in truth they were innocent members and supporters of the Capernaum Swimmers Association. This confusion arose because the club's emblem of a fish closely resembled that of the followers of Saint Paul, who incidentally, had no interest in swimming whatsoever.

It is a lie that Jesus had no possessions. An avid collector of Roman hat tufts, he would lie in wait atop walls, slice them off with a pen knife, and run away giggling. It was for this reason he was nailed to a bush.

After escaping with the bush he changed his name to Gerard Von Truffle and joined a band of travelling osteopaths. It was among this group he met and fell in love with Gerard, a beautiful Swede with massive knockers.

Business was poor. There was not enough work for 2,421 roaming osteopaths in the poorly populated desert regions. Seriously undernourished, the Gerards decided to try their luck with a group of wandering De-Pippers.

Pip removal was a slow and laborious process, especially while nailed to a bush. Whenever his girlfriend asked him to remove it, Gerard would squint his eyes and look at her suspiciously. Some months later he found several twigs in her lady bag, "I knew it!" he screamed.

Admitting the only reason she was with him was an overwhelming desire for the bush, they agreed to separate.

Depressed and lonely, he changed his name to Herman, then to Sean, back to Herman, then Graham, Dave, Eddy, Sue, Ralf and Toots, finally settling on Adolf. At an all time low, he began experimenting with tree bark.

It was during this time he met Adolf, a beautiful Swede with gigantic knockers and dangerously long toe nails. She explained that tree bark was perfectly harmless and would merely give him indigestion and haemorrhoids. "It's too late," he replied, "I'm addicted."

Wandering aimlessly around small villages and towns, he eventually found a job cleaning pig sties. While dreamily watching the porkers, an especially fat sow reminded him of his father. He resolved that day to return home.

Expecting a frosty reception, he was astonished to find his father overcome with joy. Furthermore, an enormous banquet was prepared to celebrate the return of his long lost son.

Kissing his cheek softly and taking his hand, Mr Joseph Ben Heli asked, with a firm, yet gentle tone, "Now son, what about that oak lowboy?"

Another Planet

People are different when they are in the company of different people, so the theory goes, and none more so than on the distant planet Colgatous - so named because of its sparkling white tors, peaks and rocky plateaus.

If, for example, Gertrude was chipper and bright eyed with Morris, in the presence of Charles she expressed a cool air of detached reserve.

Of course, should the three happen to find themselves in close proximity - for example within one of the many Paste Houses to be found in and around the towns and villages - if they should meet and share the same table, then you might imagine Gertrude would express a strange blend of influences, or possibly exhibit some other personality traits by which she might accommodate the differing attitudes of those present.

And this might be true anywhere else, but not on Colgatous.

On Colgatous such meetings rarely occurred, for if more than two people found themselves in close proximity they would instantly experience overwhelming nausea, followed closely by nose bleeding.

This somewhat awkward predicament has lead to some obvious social developments.

Normal accommodation must take into account the number of occupants and in large families it is not uncommon for a house to cover many acres of land, with numerous exits and entrances, annexes and floors.

Paste Houses naturally occupy very large areas due to the necessity of spacing the guests far enough apart to prevent sickness and service is only provided on a one to one basis, at regularly spaced tills.

Needless to say, crowds are unheard of, as are buses, football matches, orgies and queues.

ZETA

Zeta is a strange planet. One of the notable differences between our world and theirs is that people enter pubs and bars not to get drunk, they go to get sober.

This strange behaviour is because the natural state of a Zetan (for that is what they are called) is what we might describe as half-cut, well-oiled or bladdered.

Fortunately nature has equipped the Sixians (for that is what they are also called) with some remarkable features to accommodate their bacchanalian antics.

Sextet (for they are also known by that name) bones are thick and sturdy and their skin is tough and bouncy. Ideally suited to the inevitable accidents that beset the sozzled.

Surely, you declare, their society must be chaotic. And to that one must concede.

War, famine, disease, theft and poverty are commonplace. All the ills of a world run by drunkards. In fact a Sixer (by which they are also known) might feel quite at home on our little, blue planet.

The Time Traveller

He sat sweating in anticipation. With one press of the smooth, recessed button, Arthur Berghaussen would be cast forward into time.

What wonders awaited him, what sights?

Unfortunately Arthur had failed to include one small fact in his exceedingly complex calculations. He travelled in time, that is true. He travelled a mere decade. Safe enough, he envisaged. A small jump to acclimatise himself to the heady world of time travel. And indeed the world of one century plus Arthur's time was safe. But regretfully the planet we call Earth had moved on in more ways than mere time.

Orbiting the Sun at a rate of sixty seven thousand miles per hour, the earth and hence, his laboratory, were no longer in the place where Arthur Berghaussen had stood. Ten years on, that space was now occupied by the great vacuum of outer space.

His last words were a faint reference to his incredible stupidity, but they could not be heard. Nor could the crackle of his freezing skin as he floated in a slow orbit around the sun.

Remembering Liane

Vital and exciting, reckless and impatient, she would unscrew the marmalade two days before breakfast. That is how I shall remember Liane (spelt with the same letters as alien but in a different order).

As a child, gentle of spirit, yet horrifically violent, she understandably mistook the numerous 5th formers who gathered close, as youthful admirers, when in truth they were seeking protection from the 6th.

Admired she was though. And desired. Ravishing beauty, wit and vim combined. Though many confused the vim with a popular scouring powder, one of the first products created by William Lever, which first appeared on the market in 1904.

She, like all who live upon a solar flare, had imperfections. Incessant flatulence, the propellant force of which was comparable to the small centrifugal flow turbines utilised by recent model jet planes, was one of the more obvious. Thunderous belching another.

But she could dance. The Chicken being her especial favourite. To this she brought the manic brilliance and wild exuberance of a Pan-like goddess after a heavy night on the brown ale.

Other features include:

- 60kw output
- Thermostat
- Frost protection
- 2 heat settings
- Cool air facility
- Overheat protection

Terms & Conditions Apply.

The Peacock and the Fly

A Peacock was boasting to a fly. "Look at my fine feathers, aren't you envious? And look too at how stately and beautiful I am. You however, are no more than a filthy little fly, hated by both beast and man."

"It is true," said the filthy little fly, "we are hated by both beast and man, but when you die my kind will feast on your flesh and lay eggs in your eyes."

"I beg your pardon?" said the peacock.

"My sons will vomit on your carcass and my daughters will copulate on your putrified breast."

"What!" squirmed the peacock.

"My offspring shall dance on your decaying body and suck juice from your veins, they will spit and dance and excrete on your rotting feathers and laugh as they feast on your internal organs, they will..."

"Take that!" said the peacock as it swallowed the fly.

Hitler - The Naughty Years

An interview by
Sean Mahone's younger brother.

Good day.
Guten Tag.
How are you?
Fine, fine.
May I call you Adolf?
Ja, whatever.
I ask because during your life on earth you had many titles. Do you have one now?
Call me what you like… Adolf, Hitler, Fuhrer, Hister, Sixth Dark Lord of the Underworld, it's all the same to me.
Dark Lord of the Underworld?
Ja, ja.
You are a Dark Lord now?
I'm responsible for the deaths of 12 million people, I opened the gates to Hell, did you expect me to settle for less?
You are proud of that fact?
Ja. I could have done more.
Which brings us to the question of the Jews
Ja?
Why did you hate the Jews?
I don't hate the Jews, some of my best friends are Jews!

And yet, aren't you responsible for the holocaust, the torture and annihilation of over 6 million Jews?

They needed a homeland, I needed the cash.

I'm sorry, I don't quite follow.

We made a deal. How else were they going to get their own country? They owe me.

What kind of deal?

Countries don't grow on shrubs. The world needed a moral imperative, I gave them one. For a price. Panzers cost money. Bombs and bullets don't grow on shrubs either.

Talking of plants, you were a vegetarian, was this choice based on a moral imperative?

Of course.

A love of animals?

No, no, no, I should say it was based on an immoral imperative! Ha!

An immoral imperative?

Ja. It isn't easy being evil. It takes a lot of dedication, determination, skill. You need inspiration. Meat clogs the mind. Mind you, I did like the odd liver dumpling.

Inspiration? I presume you mean evil inspiration?

Ya, ya, ya.

From the Devil?

Ya, the Devil. Who were you thinking of? The Virgin Mary? Ha!

Do you think if you'd been a successful painter then World War II may never have happened?

You don't like my paintings?

I didn't say that.

What do you know about art? Huh? Picasso, pah! Bloody fascist.

Do you still see Eva?

Eva? Eva! Traitorous whore!

She left you?

She fucked off with Eichmann. She said I loved Blondi more.

How is Blondi?

Blondi! Don't talk to me about Blondi! Traitorous bloody bitch. She left me for a Pinscher! A bloody Pinscher. Can you believe it!

How do you fill your time these days?

I'm very busy. I have minions to command, I paint a little, I watch Eastenders.

This brings me to my main question...

Ja?

Your moustache...

Oh I see. The moustache. It's always the same with you bloody journalists, it always comes down to my bloody moustache. What's the problem? Huh? It's facial hair, it's a bloody moustache for fucks sake. Jesus! Every fucking time!

But it... it's a rather...

What? It's a rather fucking what?

Well it's… er, well it's rather an odd shape, don't you think?

Oh fuck off! Sepp Dietrich, Chuck Dukowski, Max Fleischer, they all had 'em, even Blakey had one!

Blakey?

On the Buses.

Ahh yees.

I do a turn. Do you want to see it?

Hitler proceeds to impersonate bus Inspector Cyril 'Blakey' Blake.

"I'll get you for this Butler, you see if I don't!" Ha ha ha ha, I love that guy.

The Wasp & the Bee

A Wasp was boasting to a Bee. "What poor creatures you are," he laughed, "you only have one sting and when you use it you die. Whereas we live on to sting and sting!"

"And what fools you are too, since you work all day and another reaps the fruits of your labour!"

"It is true," replied the Bee, "that we only have one sting and that when it is used we die, but for that we are respected.

"It is also true that we labour for another's gain, and for that we are prized.

"You wasps, however, are neither prized nor respected. Look, this very moment our keeper is destroying your nest!"

Bonsai !

Once upon a time, in a land not far from here, (in fact, only two streets in that direction, just turn left at the corner shop), there gathered a group of finickity plant lovers. They would meet in the town hall every third Monday of every month, every second Tuesday of every other month, three days before the last Friday of every fourth month and occasionally on the last Sunday of June.

It was their practice and passion to prune, wire, clamp and clip young trees in order to stunt their development, giving them the impression of being miniature replicas of their stately and full grown counterparts.

Occasionally they would hold competitions to determine who among their group was the most skilled. It was during one such event that a strange and mysterious lady came within their midst.

Standing only 3 foot and 6 inches tall she scuttled into the room. Her golden, curly hair bounced like the coiled plastic tubes used to support newly planted trees. In her hand she held a fine, domed terrarium, the contents of which were obscured by frosted glass.

Approaching the dwarf like creature, Mrs Elainius Truncaton, the association's president, with eyes fixed firmly on the little terrarium, ventured to ask whether she would be entering a tree. "Oi am, oi am, oi am," the weird little newcomer replied and so she was led to the registration table and enthusiastically enrolled under the name of Pipa O'Floity.

Anxious to see what lay beneath the finely patterned, frosted glass cover, the small group gathered round as she gently placed it upon the display table. Lifting the lid she revealed, to gasps of incredulity, the most delicately formed, perfectly proportioned cherry tree.

In full blossom, the specimen stood a mere 7 inches tall and exuded an odour of such exquisite nature they all moved closer to inhale the heady perfume more deeply.

At first swooning, one by one they noticed, with growing astonishment, that the tree was in fruit. Tiny red berries hung half hidden beneath each branch and at the base of the trunk a miniature woven basket sat upon what appeared to be finely cut grass, sprinkled with tiny daisies. In the basket were more glossy little berries and their sweet smell mingled with that of the blossom.

The usual questions of technique, how long, who and where, were strangely absent, entranced as they were by the trees delicate beauty.

After not an inconsiderable amount of time (45 minutes and 32 seconds to be precise) the mesmerised party were almost roused from their reverie by the sharp trill of "What would you be thinking of me little display then, now, hmm?"

Mrs Elainius Truncaton, hardly stirring and still bending over the little tree, raptly replied, "Well…

without doubt… there's no question…" adding a dreamy "Are we all... agreed?"

"Oh yeees," answered Miss Violet Calitous, in the tone of one who had just seen the vision of perfect love. "Indeeed," said another, sighing with distant memories of long forgotten cloudless days.

"Without doubt…" continued Mrs Elainius Truncaton. "You are… without doubt… yes… without… doubt… the prize… is... most… certainly… yours…" Her voice trailing off into vales of misty childhood memory.

"That's very kind," warbled the strange little woman. "Would you be tasting the little cherries now?"

A new wonder filled the eyes of the transfixed tree clippers. In unison they turned to find Pipa O'Floity smiling, her hand outstretched. In her palm they noticed a silver needle which twinkled under the harsh fluorescent lighting.

"May we?" asked Grace Reducto.

"Could we?" whimpered Roberto Minskipero while reaching out for the needle.

"You may," smiled Pipa.

Taking the needle, Roberto turned to the little wicker basket and carefully skewered one of the bright little cherries. Placing the cherry gently on his tongue he closed his mouth. The group looked on, waiting for Roberto's reaction. They didn't have to wait long, it was obvious. He was in ecstasy.

The scramble for the needle was unsightly. It was

a determined May Blarreton who prised it from Roberto's distracted grip. This didn't stop Elainius from quickly wetting the tip of her index finger and dipping it into the basket. Beatrice Muckerton had the audacity to venture further, clumsily grabbing a cherry directly from the tree. Most, however, impatiently waited for the needle before they all experienced what a passing onlooker could only describe as a Class B drug induced stupor.

A strange stillness filled the harshly lit hall. Ridiculous grins and far away stares adorned each of their faces. How long this lasted no-one knew. Minutes? Hours? Regardless, the silence was broken by the splash of Roberto's vomit on the parquet flooring and it wasn't long before the entire group was retching in unison.

Exhausted, confused and splattered with puke, the group gradually regained enough composure to notice that not only were all of their prized bonsai missing, but so too was the mysterious Pipa O'Floity and her cherry tree.

"We've been robbed!" sobbed Mrs Reducto, wiping a greasy stain off her blouse. "I'm calling the Police!" screamed Mrs Truncaton.

After a lengthy discussion revolving around the evil machinations of one Ms O'Floity, the group decided that involving the authorities was an unnecessary complication and they certainly had no desire to entangle themselves in a drug related scandal, especially since it might endanger further meetings.

In spite of their anger, they still had the residue of beautiful dreams lingering in their minds, and it was with quiet thoughtfulness that they mopped up the spuke, and slowly dispersed.

Elainius Truncaton was the last to leave. Clicking off the lights with a sigh, she left the building.

Thoughtlessly retrieving the key from her hand bag, she turned and locked the door.

Swiftly turning to walk down the neat little path to the road, she slipped, and fell. Lifting her eyes she met the glazed stare of Beatrice Muckerton's blood stained, half intact head. She screamed. Manically lifting herself from a pool of dark red blood she slipped again and looking to her feet, saw, with equal horror, they were entwined in warm, brown, stomach entrails. She kicked and rolled. Finally regaining her balance, she stared open mouthed at the sticky remains of the former Mrs Muckerton.

Behind her she heard a squeal. She turned and stared. A sixty foot tall ginger tabby was scraping its huge paws across the tiny frame of Miss Violet Calitous. "Help me!" she screamed as the giant cat rolled her flaccid body and nipped at her broken limbs.

Elainius Truncaton did not hesitate - she turned to escape back into the hall. But there was no door handle to be seen, only thick, heavily grained wood. She looked up, the handle was at least 180 feet above her head. She looked back at the cat and saw, in the distance, a human giant swing open the iron gate at the end of the path. Craning her neck upwards, it was with immense relief that she recognised her dear husband, Thomastas Truncaton, striding down the path.

Thomastas took a glance towards the cat and roughly shoed it out of his way, while Elainius, open armed, ran towards him shouting "Thomastas! Thomastas! Ohh Thomastas!"

❧

Mr Thomastas Truncaton raised his glasses. He had decided to read his newspaper in the sweet smelling, sunlit garden that his dear wife had manicured so carefully. Elainius, however, never again set foot there.

Glancing over at the row of small, well spaced trees that he had mournfully de-potted and planted six months ago, he wondered whether it was worth making one more call to the police.

The mysterious disappearance of the Crutherton Bonsai Association had made national news. Thomastas had spent many months searching for Elainius, distributing photographs, questioning neighbours and friends. All to no avail. All ten members were never seen again, distributed as they were within the bellies of various rats, birds, cats, maggots and one particularly ferocious hedgehog.

On many a lonely evening Thomastas would sit, head bowed, staring at his shoes.

If he had taken the time to check the underside of his patent leather brogues with a magnifying glass, he may have caught the glint of his wife's diamond ring and a tiny, white finger bone, embedded in the sole. But who in their right mind would do such a thing?

End of Term

Barry was nasty. If he wasn't beating the new boys he was harassing the teachers.

Mr 'Brush Head' McBrush-Head, the school's biology teacher, ascribed his disturbing behaviour to a vitamin deficiency, as Barry's diet consisted entirely of salt and vinegar crisps, which he would force from unsuspecting school children.

Miss 'Sloppy' Sloppy, the school's sociology teacher, had decided it was a result of deprived environmental conditions and the abusive nature of his upbringing. This was a fair assumption given that he was mercilessly brutalised by his mother. Indeed, Barry's earliest recollection was being forced to eat the Daily Mirror, whilst several of her paying customers bit their nails and spat them at him.

Mr 'Tatty' O'Tatty, the physics teacher, believed that his mother had been abducted by extraterrestrials and that Barry was an alien hybrid. Both Brush Head and Sloppy derided this ridiculous notion and irreverently gurgled their staff room tea whenever Tatty proposed it.

The evil spirit that controlled Barry's mind knew better.

Assigned to him at conception, her one purpose in Barry's life was to demoralise, oppress and control his every thought.

To this end Shitter, for that was her name, was given

power over several other evil spirits whose aim was to manipulate whoever was in contact with Barry. If ever Barry's peers should be near, or should even think of him, they were bombarded with suggestions of the most hideous nature. It was by these means that Barry was under a constant barrage of irritation, humiliation, aggression and depravity, both from those around him and from within. Consequently any social interaction was fraught with unseen difficulty.

Do not imagine that these deplorable attacks went unchallenged. For every suggestion of evil there was an equal and contrary idea of good. However, due to the stodgy nature of the physical world, such high vibrational impressions made little, if any, impact at all. To the good spirit that was assigned to impress such thoughts, Barry's mind resembled an overcooked and badly prepared banana bread cake: heavy, doughy and almost impenetrable.

Prior to his incarnation, Barry had gained a somewhat bad reputation and was deemed by his contemporaries to be a less than virtuous spirit whose intentions were often not of the highest order. It was hoped that he would rise above his social handicaps and develop into a mature adult. But such hopes had been constantly dashed, frustrated as they were by Shitter and her aides.

What reason could be given for her devotion to Barry's degradation? What logic lay behind her attacks? What plan? What aim or goal?

Quite simply, there was no plan. None at all. Shitter was motivated only by the sheer horror of returning to the dark spheres, from which she was temporarily released, while perpetrating her incessant crimes of oppression and disarray.

When Judge Swanley questioned Barry, there really was no sensible reason he could proffer as to why he should decide to burn down the east wing of North Wigton's School for the Blind.

Was he responsible, given the endless harassment he had borne? Was it his own will? Could he have resisted the insane urges thrust upon him?

The good spirits cry "Yes!" No one is left without the freedom to choose good over chaos. But the odds were heavy, the cards stacked. The further from heavenly influence Barry had moved, the easier it was for darkness to pervade and control his mind.

So it was that Barry Natterton, disgraced Headmaster and Religious Instructor of the semi-scorched North Wigton School for the Blind, was taken to the place from whence he came and from there was taken to a place of execution and hung by the neck until his body was dead.

Shitter was inconsolable. On the day of the fire, she had panicked. The sudden realisation that the demise of Barry meant the cessation of her earthly escapades provoked a sudden withdrawal.

She had hoped her retreat would allow Barry to see the error of his ways and return him to the practice of less life-threatening crimes. But once freed from Shitter's evil aura, he felt, for the first time, happy. To her horror, Shitter realised that her plan was having quite the opposite effect. Barry now associated happiness with arson. He danced ecstatically between the burning tables, smashed glass cabinets, ripped down posters and splashed petrol over the fire friendly chairs. All the while laughing manically.

Chaos was Shitter's forte. Forethought and planning were as alien to her as daylight was to the seventeen screaming children trapped with Barry in the burning chemistry lab.

In a last desperate attempt to avert the inevitable, she possessed the satanically inclined Maria Trouffette, guided her to the fire alarm and forced her to head-butt the glass cover.

Too late the authorities arrived. Among the dead were little Timmy Woodcock, Samantha Tuckfield and the highly flammable Gwendolin Douglas-Hamilton. Barry survived with singed eyebrows, only to be dangled three weeks later.

The good spirits were jubilant. Deep in the dark, cold shadows of the third sphere of hell, Shitter, disgruntled with the realisation that her anarchic existence had failed to secure the relief she so badly sought, decided to relinquish her evil ways and embark upon the long, hard path to redemption and, under the careful instruction of a reformed Barry Natterton, a Celestial Diploma in Planning, Order and Forethought.

A World Apart

Jane looked at Edward. Edward looked at Jane. Between them lay a five foot gap in the earths crust. The world was splitting in two.

It happened like this...

You may recall that little rat in the Ice Age cartoon. It was just like that. A little rat was trying to crack open a nut on a stone. The resulting vibrational frequency set off a chain reaction in the earth's mantel, generating a causal loop event which was amplified by the moon's gravitational pull, together with unnaturally high sun spot activity, which in turn triggered enormous electromagnetic waves that activated the world's entire stockpile of nuclear missiles. They all exploded. The resultant shockwaves penetrated deep into the world's mantel and the earth split open. Unlike the cartoon, the rat fell into a gaping chasm and was crushed to death beneath falling debris.

In any planetary catastrophe there always exists the last two people alive. In this instance it happened to be Jane and Edward Bowdernesstonsonly of 53 Rowen Mews, Barchester, Wessex.

Jane had only just returned from Tescos and Edward was watching 'A Place in the Sun' on their hi-definition, widescreen television.

As Jane reached the garden gate the earth shook, tearing down the south facing wall of their pretty red brick bungalow.

Edward turned to Jane in shock, as an enormous rent tore through their petunias, engulfed the rose bed and swallowed their delicately manicured privet hedge.

His final words, the last words ever to be spoken by man, were "Shall I put the kettle on?"

He didn't even say 'Dear'. Thoughtless bastard.

TRENDS IN PLASTIC SURGERY

Terrence, orphan, bicycle courier and lava lamp collector, aged 34 and native of Manchester, Northern England, was habitually bummed from the age of sixteen.

Terrence recalls: "I quite liked it at first, I liked the attention, but the novelty soon wore off. It hurt."

By the age of 17, Terrence had been bummed 276 times, in the main, by complete strangers.

"I didn't understand, I thought it was natural, that being bummed was part of growing up. It was only when my pregnant girlfriend made comments, about my abnormally dilated bottom hole, that I realised something was wrong."

Discovering that he didn't have to submit to the lascivious demands of practically every stranger he encountered, Terrence made a stand.

"I'd tell them that I wasn't interested but they ignored me, their eyes would glaze and they just kept bumming me. It was quite upsetting."

Angered by these relentless attentions, Terrence decided to inform the police.

"I'd had enough. My girlfriend dumped me and I'd developed piles. I went to the police but the officers in charge bummed me too."

With no one to turn to, Terrence descended into a deep depression.

"I couldn't understand it. Why me? I decided not

to wash, to make myself ugly, in the hope that it would stop."

Smelling of stale urine and wearing diamond patterned tank tops with corduroys, Terrence's problems continued.

"It made no difference, I tried everything. Sleeveless denim jackets, white socks in sandals, maternity dresses. I couldn't find a rear ended chastity belt. Nothing worked. It was then I had the idea."

Terrence made several applications to plastic surgeons for advice.

"The first consultant I saw was sympathetic but while I was being examined he bummed me."

Undeterred, Terrence was eventually introduced to Dr Audrey McRusticom.

"Audrey was my saviour. Admittedly, at first she produced a strap-on, but she did eventually decide to help me."

Audrey's intention was to stitch up the buttocks and re-route the anal passage through his left thigh.

"The main difficulty," Audrey recalled, "was resisting the urge to bum Terrence during the operation."

After a lengthy period of adjustment ,Terrence is now happily married to Sandra and is the proud a father of 2 girls.

"It was a stupid idea, a complete waste of money. I don't get bummed anymore but I suppose being thighed is slightly more tolerable."

Terrence is currently patenting a bicycle seat that accommodates crackless bottoms.

The Time Traveler's Son

"It's horrific! Outrageous! Disgusting! Inhuman!" Screamed the time traveller's son." I just don't like it."

"What! What! What's horrific, outrageous, disgusting and inhuman?" Queried the time traveller's son's occasional friend.

"I can't breath!" gurgled the time traveller's son.

"You're hyperventilating. Quick, put this plastic bag over your head!" The time traveller's son's occasional friend shouted, handing over a plastic bag.

"I don't need another plastic bag on my head! Let me take this one off." Sitting down, the the time traveller's son gasped, "The future! The damn God damned future! it's so God damned horrible."

"Sit down, tell me. What's so?" Inquired the occasionally enquiring occasional friend of the time traveller's son.

"It's the women, the damned God damned women! Boo hoo, errrgharrgh!" The time traveller's son clasped his head in hands and blubbered.

"What!? What the... Just tell me! Where have you been?" The enquiring, occasional friend inquired, enquiringly. "For the love of parsnip soup, take this pint of 75% proof potato moonshine and tell me!"

Three hours after sipping a small slurp of the moonshine, the time traveller's son regained consciousness and told his tale.

"Last week I found my mysteriously dearly departed

mysterious father's technical plans for a prototype time machine. Since I had nothing to do that day, I decided to construct the device.

"I instantly noticed there was a fatal flaw in his plans. The device would travel through time, that much was certain. But it did not travel through space! If I were to take a jaunt into any time period, I might find myself dislocated from the earth floating in the great vacuum of the cosmos!

"There was nothing for it. I employed sixteen Korean techno wizards from freelancer.com, to amend the perilous problem and wazzam, sixteen ecru payments later I had myself a fully functional functioning time machine."

The time traveller's son took a huge self congratulatory gulp of his 75% proof potato moonshine and collapsed. Three days later he awoke to continue his tale…

"I took the machine to the year 2070. I was bored. I had a time machine, what did you expect?" The time traveller's son paused, glanced at his moonshine, scratched his one remaining gonad, then continued… "When I arrived I thought things hadn't changed much, which in retrospect was to be expected, after all I'd only travelled a mere decade into the future. A small jump, I thought, to acclimatise myself to the heady world of time travel. But there was something different. Something horrific. Oh God, help me! Block this vile memory! Boo hoo, errrgharrgh." The time traveller's son wiped his eyes and continued...

"I noticed that there were no women in the year 2070, non at all. Until... Until I asked for directions from a bearded gentleman of slim demeanour. He answered in a curiously high pitched voice. The voice of woman. It was then, then I realised. I looked around and then I realised! I realised that there were women alright. But, but they all wore beards! Boo hoo, errrgharrgh.

"Confused, I asked about. I discovered it was the latest fashioon, Boo hoo, errrgharrgh. Disgusting!"

"Women wear beards in 2070?" Inquired the enquiring occasional friend of the time traveller's son.

"They don't wear beards in in 2070, they grow them!" Screamed the TT's son. "On their chinny chin chins!

"I've got to do something. I can stop this! I must warn the world! It's horrific!" The time traveller's son took a swig of his 75% proof potato moonshine and ran into the street, shouting , screaming, 'Women, women! Stop! Don't ever! Don't grow! Don't grow beards!" He then collapsed.

Two days later he woke, "It's useless." he moaned, "what's the point."

Unknown to the time traveller's son, Akiko Sakarako, fashion victim and occasional trend setter, heard his screams and decided that day, to acquire several cartons of testosterone pills.

www.ingramcontent.com/pod-product-compliance
Ingram Content Group UK Ltd.
Pitfield, Milton Keynes, MK11 3LW, UK
UKHW020216250726
13967UKWH00001B/25

9 781105 242885